MaNABeShimA ISLaND JaPaN

One island, two months, one minicar, sixty crabs,
eighty bites and fifty shots of SHochu

FLORENT CHAVOUET

TUTTLE Publishing

Tokyo | Rutland, Vermont | Singapore

The Tuttle Story
"Books to Span the East and West"

Many people are surprised to learn that the world's leading publisher of books on Asia had humble beginnings in the tiny American state of Vermont. The company's founder, Charles E. Tuttle, belonged to a New England family steeped in publishing.

Immediately after WWII, Tuttle served in Tokyo under General Douglas MacArthur and was tasked with reviving the Japanese publishing industry. He later founded the Charles E. Tuttle Publishing Company, which thrives today as one of the world's leading independent publishers.

Though a westerner, Tuttle was hugely instrumental in bringing a knowledge of Japan and Asia to a world hungry for information about the East. By the time of his death in 1993, Tuttle had published over 6,000 books on Asian culture, history and art—a legacy honored by the Japanese emperor with the "Order of the Sacred Treasure," the highest tribute Japan can bestow upon a non-Japanese.

With a backlist of 1,500 titles, Tuttle Publishing is more active today than at any time in its past—still inspired by Charles Tuttle's core mission to publish fine books to span the East and West and provide a greater understanding of each.

Published by Tuttle Publishing, an imprint of Periplus Editions (HK) Ltd.

www.tuttlepublishing.com

Copyright © 2010 by Editions Philippe Picquier

English-language translation copyright © 2015 by Periplus Editions (HK) Ltd.

Library of Congress Control Number: 2015945222

ISBN 978-4-8053-1343-5

First English-language edition
18 17 16 15
5 4 3 2 1
1508TW

Printed in Malaysia

Distributed by

North America, Latin America & Europe
Tuttle Publishing
364 Innovation Drive
North Clarendon
VT 05759-9436 U.S.A.
Tel: 1 (802) 773-8930
Fax: 1 (802) 773-6993
info@tuttlepublishing.com
www.tuttlepublishing.com

Japan
Tuttle Publishing
Yaekari Building, 3rd Floor
5-4-12 Osaki, Shinagawa-ku
Tokyo 141 0032
Tel: (81) 3 5437-0171
Fax: (81) 3 5437-0755
sales@tuttle.co.jp
www.tuttle.co.jp

Asia Pacific
Berkeley Books Pte. Ltd.
61 Tai Seng Avenue #02-12
Singapore 534167
Tel: (65) 6280-1330
Fax: (65) 6280-6290
inquiries@periplus.com.sg
www.periplus.com

Japan is so much an island that it's an archipelago.

And if you count isolated rocks, the country claims more than four thousand islands.

BUT I ONLY KNOW TWO.

It's a very meager ratio if you compare it to the three cathedrals that an average japanese tourist visits out of the two hundred that are in France. In order to compensate for this lack and to better my average, I decide to take a boat or a bridge and to meet at least one new island.

YES, but WHICH ONE?

In the japanese catalog, islands are many – some are sacred and some are gated, some are industrial and some are artificial, some are tropical and some are topical, some are mountainous and some are scandalous, some are wild and some are mild, some are atolls and some are dust bowls, and there are even islands where people fish and drink.

What luck: I don't know how to fish.

In order for my decision not to be completely a by-product of chance, I impose upon myself a few criteria: an island small in size and in the number of inhabitants, and isolated but still accessible.

In short, a real island. Better still, an island's island.

So the catalog gets shorter, and narrows itself down, and my choice hones in on the Inland Sea (SETONAIKAI), a region where villages are separated not by prairies but by ocean currents, and where bell towers are lighthouses.

It remains for me to choose between these crumbs of land the one island that is the least spoken about and to select among the four seasons the one where fish grow.

perfect, I hadn't planned anything for the summer.

TokYo, SHibuYa disTRict, HiRoo ARea, 5th fLoor.
 WithiN 7 days, I Will hAVE LEft JaPaN. ENd of tHe tRIP.
 I waNted to buY MYSelf a SQuid's TenTacle iN oRder to Keep the RhYthM,
 but they SEll it foR ¥300 PeR IOO GRaMs at HaNaMASA... KSo!
 EVeN tHoUGH the Sea is Not faR, EVeN thoUGH Less thAN A weeK aGo
 I hAd Had ENoUGH of SQuid.
  Even CaTs Got their ShaRe.

WEDNESDAY, JULY 1ST, 2009
MANABESHIMA, OKAYAMA PREFECTURE.
8 am.

9

MY ROOM

welcome to my place. I live in a telescope.

Good thing I wasn't looking for a ryokan, otherwise I'd have been disappointed. It was a former customer, enamored with the night sky, who gave them the idea of building this telescope.

BUT IT'S ALWAYS CLOSED.

SANAGI (3 miles away)

The sea

Tomato bunch (my first gift)

My ultra-sophisticated fishing gear.

About 4.5 tatami.

After bargaining about the length and price of my stay, Michiru agreed I would stay in this room they never normally rent out.

She immediately brought back a low table, a futon and fan.

CHANGING ROOM IN CASE YOU'RE GOING SWIMMING.

My friend the bucket.

SANAGISHIMA

SHIKOKU IN
THE DISTANCE

And tHis is the view
that'll be waiting for me
every morning
for 2 months.

FOR MY FIRST EVENING, i am inviTed To waTcH a movie aT THe GORi-GORi, THe "CommuniTy HaLL" in THe viLLage square. (It even has a Large sTone 鳥居 ToRi aT THe enTRance.) i go wiTH MicHiRu and Manami so THey can inTRoduce me To THe viLLagers.

PARTiALLY SHOT ON THe iSLand, in 2006. AN AuTHenTic JAPANESE RomANTic COMEdy wiTH THWARTed oR LosT LoveS FLavoRed bY DELicious SWeeT HoNEY POuRed ON Top OF SyRuP.

I THink i Love You, buT i Need To ask PeRmission FRom my mom...

Oh, aLRigHT, buT i've been waiTing FoR 34 years, yoKo.

Go on, yoKo!

AFTeR THE SCReeNiNG, THE ELdeRLY WeNT HoME To SLeEP And THE LiveLY STAyed FoR an infoRmaL LiTTLe meeTing AbouT FuTuRe PRojecTS ON THE iSLAND, GiViNG me THE OPPORTUNiTY To HONe my KNOwLEdGe OF CeRTAiN CHARacTeRS.

SEVeRaL MoViES WeRe SupposEdLY FiLMed iN MANABE, iNCLudiNG a RaTHER PoPuLaR oNE iN THE 80s ABouT BASeBALL.

BRIEF INTRODUCTIONS.

MORIYA SAN (MUNICIPAL EMPLOYEE)

Native of Manabe but Lives in Kasaoka Now. He knows all the islands Round Here.

He's A "GUIDE" among other things.

So, WHO HAS PROJECTS?

ABE SAN (CARPENTER)

KUBOTA TAKO SAN ("SUSHI MASTER")

WATANABE SAN (Middle-School Principal, since, yes, there is A middle-school!)

He Left his Fancy Tokyo Restaurant in order to come settle here with ALL his family. Just like me He, found the island on the internet. INCLUDING 3 Kids

UEMURA SAN They Just said he was Passing Through.

HIROSHI SAN comes from A family with A Long Line of Fishermen.

MORIMOTO SAN (FISHERMAN)

KATAOKA SAN (ELEMENTARY SCHOOL PRINCIPAL) ← SLEPT FOR NEARLY ALL the Meeting.

TAKAKO USUI she works FOR A (NPO) NON-PROFIT organization. She Lives IN OKAYAMA

Lives IN KURASHIKI.

HE SPEAKS A TINY BIT OF FRENCH, FROM WHEN HE BRIEFLY WENT TO THE ART SCHOOL BEAUX-ARTS de PARIS IN THE 60s.

"Là où il y a BEAUCOUP CHATS, IL Y a BEAUCOUP POISSONS"

IN FRENCH.

This is the FIRST time I draw them all so None of the Resemblances are Great (SORRY, KATAOKA SAN). BUT I have at Least A few First Names and their CORRESPONDING JOBS.

BOTH OF THEM OCCASIONALLY COME TO THE ISLAND TO MAKE THINGS HAPPEN (AND TO EAT FREE OCTOPUS).

OKAMOTO SAN ALSO WORKS FOR A NON-PROFIT. He Paints Too.

But Hiroshi is a big Romantic too, so He also pointed out to me the best "LABU-LABU" spots in KYŪSHŪ.

BECAUSE iN JaPaN, YOU ARE FREE To LoVE BuT...

Ah Oh, YES, i Love YOU MORE HERE.

... iT'S EVen BeTTeR if YOU CaN do iT iN CeRTaiN PLACes.

That's wHaT "LABU-LABU" ("Love-Love" Gone through a Japanese bLENdER) PLACes are. Famous spots where the Postcard Lends itself more To CoupLes tHaN To FamiLies (Do NOT Go To A "LABU-LABU" with your great Aunt).

SuRPRiSed by my (FoRced) inTeReST in the history of LABU-LABU spots, Hiroshi has offeRed To broaden my kNowLedGe of the LocaL LoRE.

Do you waNT to see A movie abouT tHe HiSTORY of Manabe at tHe GoRi-GoRi?

oMOSHiROi!

EXamPLes of HoT LABU-LABUs XeRoXed ON A FLYer.

But I tHiNk tHaT Practice is A LiTTLe OLD-FasHioNed. The PROOF is tHaT tHeRe's one that used To be Famous iN MaNABe.

Instead of A "History" of Manabe, it was A sort of best-of All the matsuRi that have taken pLace on the isLand since the 50s. I managed To stay Awake For TweNty years (that were all the same).

KuBoTa was tHeRe Too

HA HA. Too GooD!

Wait! NeXT, you'LL see, they ALmost broke the mikoshi.

AT ONe PoiNT, i RECOGNiZED HiRoNoBu, the HuSBaNd Ai the SaNTora.

2 HOuRs oF MaTSuRi...

1972.?

Oi Oi Oi Oi Oi

However, Manabe's Matsuri looks like it's really something. I've only seen it on video (it happens in May), but I quickly understood that it is the whole island's pride and a very decisive moment of the year.

Normally, a matsuri is like this: men from a Neighborhood, a town, a village, get dressed up, and carry a portable miniature sanctuary (the mikoshi) while shouting on top of a music loud in percussions.

the Happi, short vest

Steer Steer

BUT iN MaNabe, theY FIND iT MUCH MORE Amusing To Run Like MaDmen iN tHe steep streets.

And it usually ends up on the fishing boats that are covered in Flags for the occasion.

Jikatabi, the split-toed shoes.

Hiroshi's boat.

Comes from Osaka, where he had a small sushi Restaurant.

Landed in Manabe in 1977 and opened his dingy Place.

Black belt in Judo.

Doesn't Like Americans.

→ Lucky I'm French.

Let me introduce you to the most beautiful Haiku in All Japan:

ikkyu san

BiRU? SHŌCHŪ?

The world according to him.

Has a marked Preference for SHŌCHŪ, (wheat-based distilled alcohol).

In the country of studied Refinement, of coDified politeness, of Restrained human emotions and Noble social codes, Ikkyu san has the distinction of being the perfect and generous (albeit grumpy) Provincial inn-keeper. To observe this, you only have to walk slowly in Front of his inn.

The only one on this island, at the port entrance.

COME HERE ...

With him, it always starts like this...

...and ends up like this

COME ON NOW, FINISH YOUR SHŌCHŪ!

Sometimes he cuts it with iced tea. We're not savages.

SHOCHU IICHIKO
下町のナポレオン
むぎ焼酎
25
いいちこ
1800.ml

ALCOHOL LEVEL

FAMILY SIZE

21

22

The REGULAR MembeRs

DAILY MEMBER

Day-GLo Cap Guy

He doesn't talk much, but He's ALways there. FoR him, CoNversation is Like teLevision oR A movie. He doesn't say A word and Nods FRom time To time (Counting Points?).

HA HA

He often Gets the PLace in the back. It Looks as though he Likes being stuck theRe.

I think He is - oR was- A FisheRman.

He aLways Has A sLight smile.

He has A smaLL CaR, aLways PaRked iN FRoNt of the joint.

WEEKLY MEMBER

Skinny Guy

He's ofteN oN the bench outside.

He's A kind of Gate-keePeR.

Sometimes He Comes in to Check that eveRyone's dRinking theiR shōchū.

YuP. VeRy skinny.

MONTHLY MEMBER

GReasy-HaiRed Guy

As He's A FisheRman, He's theRe OccasionaLLy (meaning several Times A week).

He has aN "extended" FamiLy and i'm still Not suRe who's the bRotheR-in-Law's Cousin's soN's bRotheR.

He's Nice but i DoN't ReaLLy Like him Leafing through my dRawings. The FiRst time i saw Him, He feLL off his stool and HuNg oN To my Notebook.

As aN OCCasioNaL boNus, we get the buRPing GRandma.

BuRRP

THE VERY GOOD SAUCE, MADE UP OF 12 MYSTERIOUS INGREDIENTS, OF WHICH i ONLY RECOGNIZE "LEMON"...

IKKYU-SAN DOES HIS CHEMISTRY.

and there you are!

DIP.

SECRET NOODLE LABORATORY.

It's not overdoing it to say that it's MORE Refreshing than A beer.

MUCH THINNER THAN UDON.

SHAVINGS OF DRIED NORI

IN ORDER TO SAVE MONEY, i TOLD myself i would eat oNLY oNE meal A day (DINNER AT the SANTORA).
But Ikkyu-san invites me FOR LUNCH several Times and won't LET me pay (when NONE of his Fishermen Friends are around).
The oNLY way i've found To pay without Him getting upset is To HIDE COINS oN the table whiLE He's Cooking.

FROM NOW ON, I CAN Be CONSIDERED TO HAVE MY MEMBERSHIP CARD.

WEEKLY ONLY.

SŌMEN,
a REAL SUMMER dish.
(Because SHŌCHŪ Can't provide ALL YOUR NUTRIENTS)
Like udon, these noodLes Are wheat-FLOUR based.
And like udon, you can eat them Cold.
with ice Cubes Right oN Top.
OR dipped in iced sauce.

KAMPAI!

SANTORA

NAMAE: CHAVOUET FLORENT
DOKO: FRANCE
MEMBER: n° 0015

IKKYU SAN

24

The Nakamuros

Big Family, happy Family

OSAMU — I see him less often than the rest of the family because he doesn't work on the island. He leaves with the first boat (around 7 am) and comes back on the last (around 6 pm).

I got to know them quickly since one of Atsumi's jobs is running the Kaisōten, the boat Ticket office. Their House shares a wall with the office (which is at the Dock's entrance) and is Right in front of ikkyu san's place.

ATSUMI — They beat Hiroshi-the-Fisherman's Record by having 5 children. Unfortunately not enough to Reverse the island's demographic trend. Anyway, they only moved to the island one year ago.

TAKUMI (age 15)

KAZU (age 2)

AN (3 months) The youngest inhabitant of the island (and 4 brothers to put up with)

While I was looking for edible Alms walking by ikkyu san's door (strangely He wasn't there), Atsumi invited me to drink A beer in exchange for A drawing of baby An.

WATARU (age 8) Rinko's friend.

SORA (age 4) — They played the drums at the last Matsuri.

This is the kind of deal that i like. Once the drawing was done, Osamu scanned it.

In order To print it on Plastic Fans.

Hello An Chan Trademark ©

About $100 Rent. i understand why they settled here!

THE NAKAMUROS' HOUSE

真鍋島は心のふるさと またのおこしをまっています

The island's ONLY public phone.

Waiting Room and Parcel depot.

This is where you disembark.

Restrooms

You buy Tickets Here To get To Neighboring islands (Shiraishishima, Kitagishima, Mushima...) or the "Continent" (Honshu).

YUTAKA HAMANO Aluminum-can CLERK. He also grows GOYA

type of VERY bitter Cucumber with Leprosy.

Cold Coffee

The way inTo Honmura, the main village, and Toward the Gori-Gori.

The Famous KAISŌTEN (回送店) (OR KAISOUTEN)

This is one of the FIRST drawings i did in public, and because I'd chosen the busiest place on the island, I became known to a lot of people in just one morning.

管理室　　　資料展示室

ATSUMI'S COUNTER-OFFICE.

The MaNaBe STaMP

MaMiKo →

WaiTiNg PaRceLs

In MaNaBe, wheN YoU'Re dRawiNg OUTSide And it's RaiNiNg, theRe's No maLL oR Coffee sHoP wHeRe YoU Can Take sheLTeR. BuT YoU Can Go iNSide the KAISŌTEN

→ AfRaid oF dRowNiNG.

I've dRawN heR BadLy.

ATSuMi gave me an AnTi-mosquiTo device and 2 onigiRi Rice baLLs to RewaRd me foR this stRange PerspecTive I'm making up.

They'Re NoT Dumb. WheN iT RainS They Go inSide HouseS, just LiKe us.

This Guy is A TouRist. He Came HeRe because His Last Name is "MaNaBe." He TeLLS me it's the Name of many A Japanese.

27

FOLLOWING THE drawing on the preceding page, when she HAD PLENTY of time to discover that she figured PROMINENTLY, she fell in love with me.

→ TO TAKE WITH OR WITHOUT A GRAIN OF SALT, I KNOW NOT, I'M STILL WONDERING.

YOUHOU!

BONZOUL!

SHE STARTED WAITING FOR ME IN THE MORNING, IN FRONT OF THE PORT...

...AND TO DEMAND THAT I DRAW HER AGAIN, PORTRAIT STYLE.

HIROSH'KUN WHO'S MAKING FUN OF ME.

me.

Yes, OKay then...

183°F CONCRETE.

WHICH I DID, UNWILLINGLY.

BUT IT WASN'T ENOUGH. SHE CONTINUED TO FOLLOW ME, TO WANT MORE DRAWINGS, TO OFFER ME COOKIES AND A PLASTIC RING.

LABU LABU!

THAT'S WHEN MY SAVIOR INTERVENED...

SCHLOP SCHLOP

REGULAR, DRY SOUND FROM HIS FLIP-FLOPS.

OOOH PROFESSIONAL!!!

ALAIN DELON!

← NO NECK.

SHIMURA SAN

He used to be a very good fisherman (or so he says). "Used to be" because out of his 3 boats, one was pulverized by a storm ("BA!!" as he says), one is "stuck" in Kasaoka, and the last one has broken down. Anyway, He doesn't have a license. So now, He ekes a living from fields He has sort of everywhere on the island. But His tractor gave out. There. That's Shimura san's story.

WATCH that Doesn't work.

70s PaNTS in PerfecT CoNDiTioN.

His Dad is Hospitalized in Kasaoka while His mom still Lives in the Family House.

When i decide to dedicate Him this Page, i've known Him for about a week. But He's the one i've seen the most. In general. He's Here From the beginning of a drawing To its end. with sometimes a few back-and-forths To his House in order To bring me stuff. In other words, He's always there, and Finds me every time (even Hidden deep in the woods).

In any case, it's thanks To him and an improvised fishing expedition (He said He knew the good spots) that Mamiko stops Harassing me.

OH, come on, Mamiko! Don't You see we're Fishing?

Yep, it's serious.

BUT He Has To Do me a Drawing.

We've caught absolutely Nothing

DRIED FUGU

I can already at this stage make a List of words that come up again and again in His conversations:

- ALAIN DELON
- RENOIR
- LE~~XL~~ ← No, ActuaLLY it's "LouVre"!
- WORLD CHampion
- MOVIE STAR
- Jeanne d'arc
- Napoléon
- PROFESSIONAL
- SORBONNE

...
List To be Completed

He Talks to me ALL the time, SHimura san, and i DoN't understand a word. He Doesn't mind.

MORNING SCHEDULE

①A It's 9 am, the "boss", South Port's cat gang's chief, finds it a good reason to sleep.

①B The ship comes in and blows twice.

①C This is the signal for Atsumi who darts out of her house.

②A She barely manages the first turn, but takes it too sharply. The ship blew 12 seconds ago already.

②B Hirosh'kun and "Mister Gloomy※" are already hard at work, on the pontoon, ready to receive packages and travelers alike.

②C The "cool deckhand" comes to tie up the boat and prepare the merchandise.

②D The last 15 Yards for Atsumi

③A Loading mail for the mainland and unloading Manabe's. "Mister Gloomy" takes charge of the wheel-barrow and Atsumi checks the tickets.

③B Nature calls Ikkyu san and he runs to the public restrooms that he's completely colonized, in front of his house.

④ The little crowd ("Mister Gloomy", Hirosh'kun and Atsumi) bring back all the packages to the Kaisouten (in that order, from heavier to lighter).

⑤A Hironobu arrives by motor scooter while singing, to see whether there's anything for the Santora.

⑤B Dominique the Crab finds the day has begun well since he's managed to avoid the scooter.

⑥A The "cool deckhand" has 15 minutes in front of him before going back to Kasaoka. Plenty enough to empty an iced coffee can and to have a smoke.

⑥B During the 3 minutes and 41 seconds of this episode, the "boss" has journeyed 15 inches. A good reason for a nap.

※ Mister Gloomy because he never talks to anyone. A pure islander who has the peculiarity of having green eyes.

※ He often waves from his boat. ←

This is the mooring for the taxi-boats that take you wherever you want, whenever you want. ⚠ Still, it's ¥10,000 each way.

※※ What? Is he there already?

FONG FONG

Hideki KURATA Manabe's Crusader

ABUNAI.

For him, everything is "ABUNAI" (dangerous). Snakes, hornets, the sea, the sun, the uneven ground...

For reasons I don't know (punishment? hazing? internship? challenge?) KURATA SAN, rookie cop from OSAKA, got sent to MANABE in order to take charge of the island's only KOBAN two years ago.

While one can question the pertinence of installing a police station here where everyone knows everyone and where the only crimes committed are the throwing of cigarette butts in the ocean and IKKYU san's tendency to convert people to alcoholism, there's a lot of amusement to be had in seeing our rookie city cop a little lost in his new universe (conversations with the fishermen too short, ignorance of the local fauna...)

I sometimes see him killing time at this desk (instead of killing YAKUZA) in his native town.

He has, of course, brought his whole family to the island and, as order does not always rule in the household, you sometimes see him trying to comfort his kids with long rides along the harbor.

SUMIKO

HARUNOSUKE

KONOSUKE

They cry all the time

ABUNAI?

OLD boat cabin

Hideki is another person who is very thoughtful. When I decided to draw his KOBAN (from the first day, he insisted I do it), I started like this and 15 minutes later, I was like this.

A CHURCH?
A SCHOOL?
A LIGHTHOUSE?

NO,
a KOBAN
OF COURSE

← Machine-gun turret?

ASTONISHINGLY
NEW
building,
(i estimate
it's 6-8
years old)

The KURATA
FAMILY
Lives IN
THE whole
OF THE
back
OF the
House.

Japan's
disgusting
Criminals.

EACH TIME
I Go by, Hideki Gives
me A soDa. it's A bit
the same idea As
with ikkyu san
and His bar.
(in this Case, rePlace soda)
with SHŌCHŪ of course.)

33

34

A fish out of water.

So we get to a temple, located between 2 villages, on a hill. I understand that

Hachiman-sama is a god

of fishing there are plenty of gods of fishing, and of war.

Most important and oldest temple on the island (but not the biggest).

He's actually one of the most famous gods in Japan. He is so fabulous that the Shinto folks and the Buddhists share him. When we arrive, there are already about fifteen people.

The ceremony can start.

STOP!

BABY TEMPLE

Of course you take off your shoes.

You go in and you light candles.

Then they give out cushions... (ZABUTON)

THE CUSHION SUPERINTENDENT

WHAT THE HELL'S GOING ON?!

... and finally we get settled...

Ikkyu san is (A sort of) Monk!

In any case, he is the master of the Ceremony. The Ceremony is actually pre-recorded on audio tape. You only have to push a button and the Ritual can start.

TRY "PLAY" just to see.

← The Habit Maketh the Monk.

WAIT, WAIT, I'LL START HACHIMAN. THERE.

WHERE is SHINTO FM AGAIN?

For the moment, everyone stays put, we do nothing but Clap at Regular intervals.

CLAP CLAP

Ikkyu san is settled in Front of everyone.

MMMMF

At a moment that only He decides, ikkyu san Gathers together all his karma so He Can Get up.

→ KNEE CRACKING.

It's benediction time.

We've Lost most of the kids Already.

← COMA.

i AM DISTRIBUTING the GOD!

HE'S NOT YET sobered up and HE Has to Lean on people sometimes.

With His super-Twig, He touches everyone's head.

THERE!

CLAP CLAP

✗ End of the music and of the FIRST Part.

Hey. Even the French guy, Come on.

But it's NOT over. Ikkyu san takes out A New weapon, A golden super stick.

i HAVE the GODS' POWER!

And HERE we go again, He blesses everyone.

SUPER HACHIMAN!

THERE, YOU'RE HACHIMAN Too.

CLAP CLAP

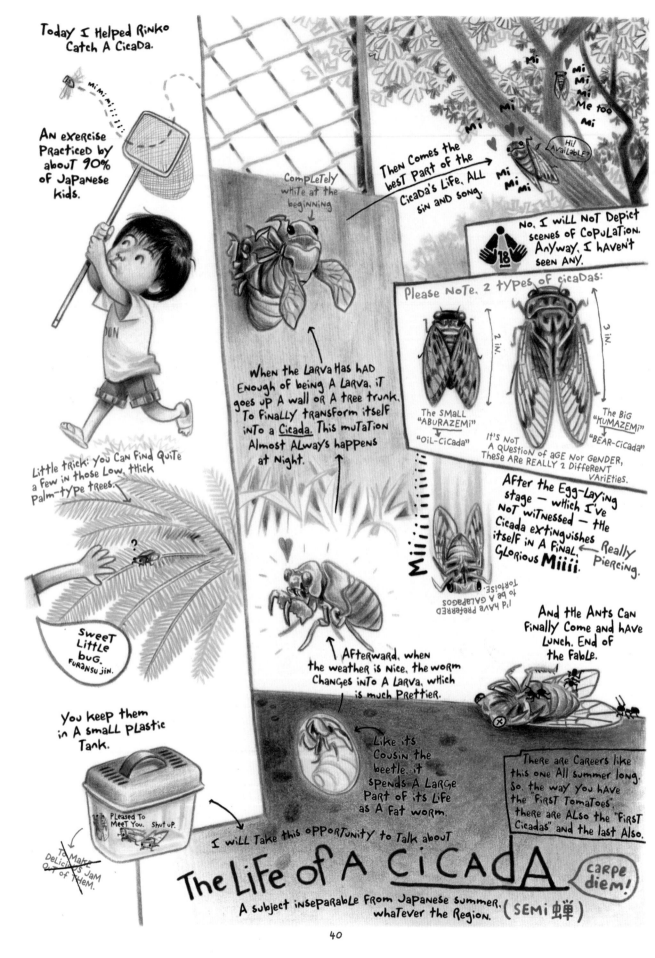

This is MR. TECHNOLOGY

(His Real Name is Morimoto san.)

Thus Renamed because of His Electronic Gadgets Collection. Rather Astonishing For A man this age and From this island.

↑ There are many "Morimotos" on The island; I get A bit Confused.

In a way, He's the most modern man on Manabeshima.

Êtes-vous Français?

Bonjour.

Voulez-vous Boire Quelque Chose?

Merci

I Had moving A Conversation with his French "Everyday Phrases" Translator.

A Very Quiet Gramps who often Harbors A slight smile.

→ He's also got A scooter.

The First Time i met Him, He Took A Picture of me with His Phone and went away.

FLASH!

He Came back A Few minutes later...

...And gave me the PHOTO He'd Just Printed.

He Now knows i understand Japanese Poorly and so He talks To me very Little, Not Like the other Locals (Shimura san For example) who Chat To me as if i were A Native.

International Artist

I believe this is "MisteR GLooMy's" House. To be Checked.

AltaR

Gas-PoweRed

Toward the School

(株)阪本熊治郎商店
☎ (代表) 2-4151
(工場) 2-4091
プロパンガスナガス器具十配管工事

FouNd oNLy the Head. He Must hAVe Left the Rest at the Coat-Check.

The GORI-

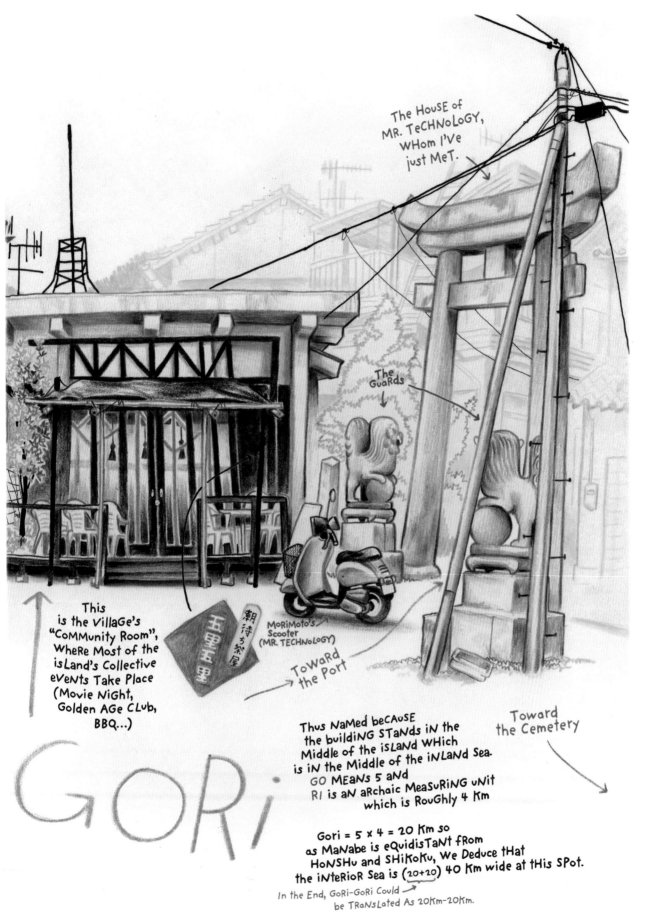

The HOUSE of MR. TeCHNoLoGY, WHom I'Ve just MeT.

The GuaRds

This is the VillaGe's "COMMunity Room", WheRe Most of the isLand's Collective eVeNts Take Place (Movie NiGht, Golden AGe CLub, BBQ...)

潮待ち茶屋

五里五里

MoRiMoto's Scooter (MR. TECHNoLoGY)

ToWaRd the Port

Toward the Cemetery

GoRi

Thus NaMed beCAUSE the buildiNG STaNds iN the Middle of the isLAND WHich is iN the Middle of the iNLaND Sea. GO MEANs 5 aNd RI is aN aRchaic MeasuRiNG uNit which is RouGhly 4 Km

Gori = 5 x 4 = 20 Km so as MaNabe is eQuidisTaNt fRom HoNSHu and SHiKoKu, We Deduce tHat the iNTeRioR Sea is (20+20) 40 Km wide at tHis SPot.

In the End, GoRi-GoRi Could be TRaNsLated As 20Km-20Km.

47

A SWEET LITTLE THING THAT IKKYU SAN ENJOYS: EATING HIS CAT'S HEAD.

MARO?

?

He REALLY catches Him by The Leg.

OH, YES, i do LOVE YOU too.

ROUIN RROUIN

SLURP!

The HEAD goes in ENTIRELY.

THE COUNTRY OF bLUE-TAiLED LiZARDS.

Found on the GROUND:

Piggy-Bank

100

DAKARA

Cat of the day:

SMALL CARDBOARD box YOU FiND ReguLARLY aT THE ENTRANCE TO THE PORT, WHERE PLANTS, FLOWERS, FRUITS, and VEGETABLES ARE offeRED ACCORDING TO THE HARVEST.

JuST As with the Cicadas, it's impossible To Talk AbouT Japanese summers without menTioning

HANA-Bi (FireWorks)
花火

Good Timing, because I meT A dozen sTudents from OKAYAMA University who Came To the SANTORA (which is oPen Now) For the weekend. (buT there's still No one DuRing the week.)

They Came ALL the way From KASAOKA by Jet-ski and decide to have A HANA-Bi FoR A Classic evening's EnterTainment.

No MusiC, Yeah No LiFe! MAN!

This Guy is KioHei the Group's Chief, 21, DJ in Osaka After His Pro-soccer Career was Cut short by An inJuRy.

YuP, Kiohei hAs indeed PuT the Equivalent of A Dozen Bison III in his briefs.

AAAH iTai!*

* That hurts.

It Tickles Him A biT buT he Finds it FuNNy.

When you're 15 or older, HANA-Bi are A great PReteXt to Fool aRound. Especially if theRe ARe girls watching.

B E A C H

iTai

Then Kiohei was punisHed by A bomb under his shirt. This is the scene, with veRy Little exaggeration:

A iTai!

BuT it made the GiRls LaugH.

He ended uP PLunging in the sea.

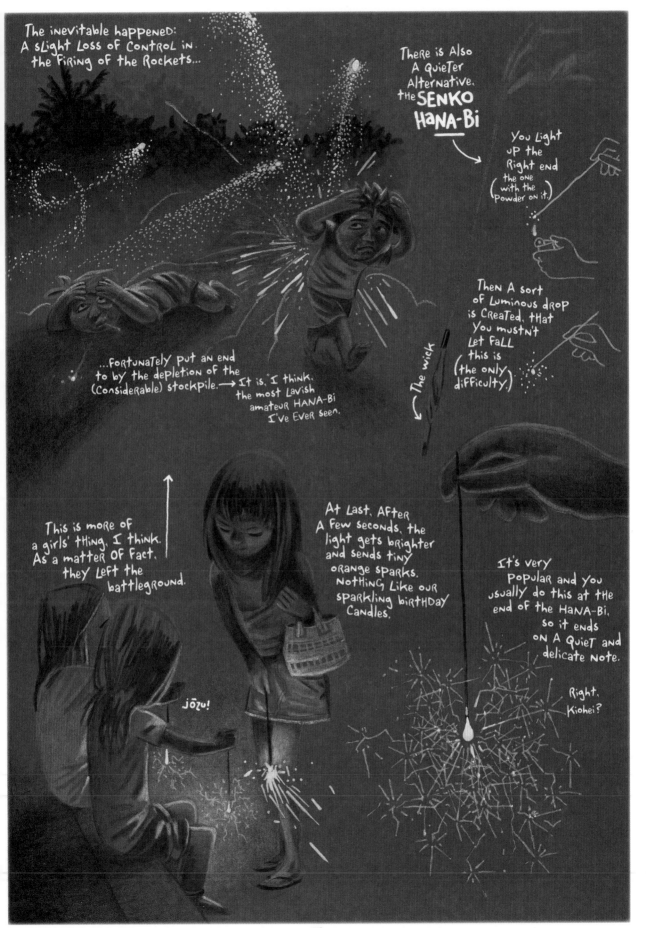

The inevitable happened:
A slight loss of control in
the firing of the rockets...

There is also
a quieter
alternative,
the **SENKO**
HANA-BI

You light
up the
right end
the one
(with the
powder on it.)

...fortunately put an end
to by the depletion of the
(considerable) stockpile. → It is, I think,
the most lavish
amateur HANA-BI
I've ever seen.

Then a sort
of luminous drop
is created, that
you mustn't
let fall
this is
(the only
difficulty.)

The wick

This is more of
a girls' thing, I think.
As a matter of fact,
they left the
battleground.

At last, after
a few seconds, the
light gets brighter
and sends tiny
orange sparks.
Nothing like our
sparkling birthday
candles.

It's very
popular and you
usually do this at the
end of the HANA-BI,
so it ends
on a quiet and
delicate note.

Right,
Kiohei?

JŌZU!

51

FOUND ON THE BEACH: FAKE BENTO SEAWEED.

"TOMOE-MON" (KAMAKURA PERIOD).

IN THE RUINS OF A HOUSE.

オロナミンC ドリンク

FUNNY BAG.

CAT OF THE DAY:

ROOF TILE →

MOM...? MOSH...?

FISH CAUGHT BY HAND!

IT LOOKS LIKE A

ACTUAL SIZE

SPOTTED YELLOW FISH FINGERLING

AFTER INQUIRY HOWEVER, IT TURNS OUT IT IS ACTUALLY A SMALL MABEIKA

WEIRD AND UNKNOWN PLANT.

Reizo San

Manabeshima's Hard drive

It's very simple: at Reizo San's, the newest thing is his house, built at the beginning of the Meiji era (end of the 19th century). Like him, it's in a very good shape.

Well, here, for page-layout reasons, I have him walking upon the roof of his house, but Reizo San is actually a very sensible person.

It's a real unofficial museum, always open. You can go in the little garden reception area at any time, any way you want. ↓

Tree from Portugal, over 200 years old. ↑

entrance →

AT REIZO SAN'S.

tinue

his

day

Old MANABE PHOTOS

ANCESTOR OF THE TV?

THIS IS HIS CALLIGRAPHY STUDIO. He Loves it.

Besides. He writes Everywhere.

RICE RESERVES.

SHOE PARKING.

GENKAN

STONE

SHIKIDAI

UMEBOSHI (SAVORY PLUMS)

Cupboards FOR Vegetable and Fruit Preserves. THERE ARE too Many

YOU COME IN THIS WAY.

Thanks to Michiru, I finally got an explanation about these remnants of metallic structures strewn here and there on the island, more or less covered by vegetation. They were for electrical wiring over old KIKU fields. Kiku (the imperial chrysanthemum) used to be a speciality of Manabe and the surrounding islands. And if you lit them up, they'd bloom quicker (?). No, not very economical.

in the 50s.

That's actually the reason the industry collapsed. Other islands further south (Okinawa and places) started the same business with no need for field lighting.

A low-cost kiku in other words.

Nowadays, there are almost no kiku on Manabe. Only the structures remain.

A beautiful kiku.

I've seen photos of the Kiku era (at Reizo san's and at the Santora) but none show the fields lit at night. It must have been rather pretty though...

From my sensitive and poetic imagination.

It's gone from imperial flowers to empire of the plants.

58

GRANNYMOBILE OR GRANDMOTHER'S CART.

Probably the most common vehicle on Manabeshima. It's used as a walker, as a stool and as a cooler by the granny.

Here is a great example with Ikkyu san's friend.

Customized with plastic bags and umbrella.

Brake. In case you're going too fast.

Narrow, lightweight and all-terrain, it's actually a device very suited to the streets here. (except when there are stairs.)

WHAT'S SHE GOT IN THERE?

INCENSE (KATORI SENKO)

WATER (O MIZU)

A TOMATO

A CAT? A PLAUSIBLE HYPOTHESIS.

I didn't choose the latest model, but the most representative of the local fleet.

if you see several parked in front of a house, it means grannies are meeting.

FOUND ON THE BEACH.

AND FOR GRANNIES
iN MORE of a HURRY, THeRe's
The **MINI-CaR!**
The MISSING LINK BeTWEEN The
LAWN MoWeR aND
the AuToMoBiLe.

I'd ALReady spotted it
once withouT having The
time To dRaw it. ShimuRa
saN helped me Track it
down. It beLongs To
HiSAKO ARaYAMA,
a gRanny who Lives at
The NoRTH end of
iwatsubo PoRT.

A SINGLE
dOoR Which
iS oN THiS SidE.

PLASTiC
WiNdshieLD

4 FEET

TANK CAP.

最大搭載人員4人

ABBEY

FibeR Body

3 FEET

↑
THE
VAGABOND's
BiTe MARK?

6 FEET

A gift FRom SHimuRa:
Cookies FiLLed with ANko
(Red beaN paste, wHich
makes up 90% of
Japanese desseRts.)

WHiLe I was doing this dRawing, SHimURA Told me His bRotHeR was "Dead FRom ALCoHoL." *BA!"

LET'S OPEN THE CAN

It would HAVe been FUN iF it Had been amphibious. I'm acTuaLLy CeRTaiN it FLoats.

THE BATTERY (EASY To CHANGE)

THE GeaRS (FoRWaRd and BACKWaRd)

PLASTiC FLoWeRS

The tRuNk is A PLastic tub.

The ENGiNe's under tHis bit.

VENTiLATioN DoN't DRiVE THRoUGH ANY PuddLeS.

A SiNGLE PeDAL So YoU ONLY BRaKe WitH tHE HAND BRaKe?

FOR 1 PeRSON ONLY.
(OR 3 JapaNeSE GRANNieS)

This dRawing was diFFicULt to PRodUCe siNce it was done wHiLe staNdiNG uP To PeeR iN FRom the side window (and wHiLe ResTiNG my PeNCiLS oN the RooF).
I woULd HAVe Liked SHimURA saN to be my easeL, but I HAd No idea How To say easeL.

61

CAT GANGS

Black book of whiskered small-time delinquents.

KINGPIN'S GANG.

THE BACKUP

6 or 8 members, all adults and submissive to the super boss, the "Kingpin", the island's toughest cat. It's also in this gang that you find "Fleabag", the island's weakest.

THE A-DOCKS GANG.

5-8 members. Kittens, couples. Weakened by the recent loss of a member (by drowning).

THE TOWN GANG.

VERY YELLOW

How many members? They don't know themselves. Hang out in the vegetable patch in front of the house with the tree (page 93) and in a nearby alley. All very lazy. They all know my drawings.

THE B-DOCKS GANG.

Between 5 and 10 members. Hard to say. But several kittens. New blood in other words. but rather disorganized. To each his fish. Sleep regularly aboard the boats.

THE HIPPIES

Between 12 and 15 members, more or less from the same family. Have questionable sexual and social morals (incest, (pedophilia) swinging) ... They all squat at the house of a granny that lives on the outskirts of the village, up a hill. Slightly marginalized gang.

CONFLICT ZONES

And no UN peacekeeping force in operation

 MARO, Ikkyu san's cat. Only cat to have a legit owner. Manages to have good relationships with the A-Docks cats while keeping his own small territory. (The bar's hallway, the Kaisōten...).

 SOURCES OF FOOD.

Leftovers from the occasional barbecues at the Gori-Gori.

Bowl of Udon provided every day by the granny next door to ikkyu san (on the right). Exclusively reserved for Kingpin's gang.

VEGETABLE GARDEN LEXICON

EBOLA CUCUMBER

The Famous <u>GOYA</u> Bitter Cucumber that's difficult to Appreciate if You're Not an OLD Japanese Guy. Here, they dry it → or they Make it iNTo Jam (I've never Tasted it.)

<u>RINGO</u> APPLE

<u>ICHIGO</u> Les Fraises Strawberries strangely Ripe (2ND HARVEST?)

<u>ICHIJIKU</u> FiGs (NOT Ripe Yet)

<u>KAKI</u> Persimmons. Not Ripe Yet either.

FOR GRATING

<u>DAiKON</u> WHiTe Radish

Casting error

<u>SHISO</u> Decorative Leaf in various dishes. (A herb?) It's very Good. It Looks LiKe A poison ivy Leaf.

ORdiNary Zucchini.

<u>URi</u> Large Yellow MeLon.

<u>DAIDAI</u> Japanese ORange. Never Ripe, ↳ OR Rather, Never sweet.

<u>UME</u> Plum. The Crows have Priority.

<u>NASHi</u> Pear.

There ARE LoTs iN MANABe: You CAN HeAR TheM FaLL ON TiN RooFs oR eveN oN THe CATs.

Thick skin.

TOMATOes, someTimes in bunches, are the most Common Fruit on Manabe.

<u>MOMO</u> Peach. ONLY A Few Trees Here. → RECOGNIZABLE becAuse the FRuiTs ARe WRAPPED uP

SpoTTed Just in time. AND DOES NOT LOOK LiKE THE REGULAR JAPANESE PEAR.

<u>NASU</u> This Eggplant is smaller AND Rounder than the European Eggplant. ↓ VERY POPULAR. Especially in Tempura.

KABO CHA

Pumpkin

<u>KYABETSU</u> Cabbage → PlenTiful

<u>iNGEN</u> Bean

Bell PePPer VERY LiTTLE CONVERSATiON

DiRECTORY OF SCARECROWS iN USE:

AQUARiUS

APPARENTLY THe BiRds HeRE DoN'T LiKE Shoes.

OR PLASTiC tubs.

OR MuSic.

What's MoRe, theY'Re SuPeRSTiTiOuS.

HARAJUKU

i see HeR going fishing every morning.

SHIBUYA

HAD A HAIRCUT →

A LIGHT INTRODUCTION TO SHŌGI

Seeing Ikkyu san playing with WATARU (the NAKAMURO boy) gave me an interest in this game that Resembles Chess. The main differences are that the pawns can win "grades" (and so Additional moves) if they reach enemy territory. (The notion of Territory is important Too.) Another Critical difference, you can Re-use a pawn lost by your opponent. That's why the pieces have no color, only a direction (Corresponding to their side). There's a KING but no Queen.

(the GOAL is to PUT HiM iN CHECK.)

(REPLACED by GOLD and SILVER GENERALS.)

COMMUNIST GUERILLA, SECT, TERRORIST CELL... **PLAYER 1's side**

SWITZERLAND, BENELUX **NEUTRAL TERRITORY**

GOVERNMENT FORCES, U.N. **PLAYER 2's side**

The **KING** (1)
1 SQUARE IN ALL directions.

The **Basic PAWN** (9)
1 SQUARE FORWARD.

The **SILVER GENERAL** (2)
1 square in all directions EXCEPT BACKWARD and SIDEWAYS.

The **BISHOP** (1)
ALL Squares diAGONALLY.

The **LANCER** (2)
ALL SQUARES FORWARD. (EXCEPT if THERE'S an ObsTACLE)

The **KNIGHT** (2)
2 SQUAREs FORWARD AND 1 to THE SIDE (LefT or RighT)

The **Rook** (1)
ALL the SQUARES EXCEPT diAGONALS (REVERSE OF the bisHOP)

The **GOLD GENERAL** (2)
ONE SQUARE IN ALL diRECTIONS EXCEPT BACKWARD DIAGONALS.

This is what I could gather by watching WATARU Getting Hammered And with A few explanations from IKKYu san. BuT i doubt this is enough To win your First Game.

Cat of the day:

THIS MORNING, it's KAGURA

Sort of traditional Japanese theater, set up in the school/Hair dressing/meeting Room in IWATSUBO

Sort of miniature Gori-Gori

TWICE A YEAR.

GoD #1

demon (this much is obvious)

GoD #2

OUCH

HiRoshi's kids.

Colleague who keeps the beat and shouts from Time To Time.

Skinny Guy From ikkyu san's.

Several possible weapons.

The theater Company (4 People) spent the whole summer Performing From island to island. They're only there For A day.

DiRTY Layabout!

So, You'Re Evading Taxes?

OUCH! Take it EASY TAKESHi.

The show Lasted About an Hour during Which Two Gods spent their time killing, killing again, and Re-killing again A demon Who Can't be that evil because He Really gets beaten up.

A bit on the Light side FOR A script but it makes you want To be in it.

ANALYSIS of tHE Demon's HeaD Moves:

Goes up slowly.

Quick side Nodding.

ON MY WAY TO THE SANTORA:

GNNN...

MFE!...

MICRO GRAMPS.

May i HeLP You?

?

dōzo.

MFE...

I've NeveR MANAGED to heLP A JAPANESE PERSON. ESPECIALLY NOT AN ELDERLY ONE.

SEEN TODAY:

(AHA!) SHimuRA san's FAMOUS LAST boat. In REALITY, it's NOT bRokEN down. It's Just A dinghy.

EveRy day i ask HiRoshi – ARe you going Fishing?, and Today He answeRed that he was Going To HeLP his FRiends dig FUKUYAMA PoRt (NeXt to KASAOKA) in oRdeR FoR Australian iRON CaRgos to be able to go through. Because iRON is good.

FUKUYAMA PORT

Digging buddy

BARGE

Buddy

Stop! we can't through! Jo

HiRoshi's boat

Really?

IKKYU san sLEEPING.

HiRONOBU'S joke of the SUMMER:

May I hAve the SHŌYu ?

SHŌYU...

show me...

SHŌYU TOGETHER...

NATURALLY

72

ALL the time i was drawing, Shimura san listened to a "very important" game for Osaka's baseball team.

One of the numerous kami hidden here and there on the island.

15番国分寺

MORIJI SAN
MISTERPHOTO

Since she doesn't know Him VERY WeLL, Atsumi (with WATaRu) Takes The oPPoRTunity To Accompany us and Pay Him A visit also.

The same Two people who introduced me to Reizo san this time invite me to MoRiji san's. And MoRiji san's passion is PHotoGRaPHy. He's been doing it since He was 18. He's Now 88. So it's been A Nice Even 70 YeaRs of PHotos.

MoRiji san is PaRT of the SANToRA FamiLy (by MaRRiage, that's aLL i know...) so theRe's Quite A Few PictuRes of Rinko Chan in His House!

COMPLETELY coPied.

He must Have TakeN A Ton of oLD PHotos that CouLd Have informed me about the isLand's past but He oNLY sHows us Recent aLbums.

LoTS OF MiddLE SCHOOL CLASS PHotoS.

His LaRge studio (I've NeVeR seen iT)

His HOUSE

His GaRden (WeLL kept)

His LittLe studio (That i've gLimpsed)

The RiVeR (EVeRYone's.)

74

MINISTRY of SILLY HATS:

THE WEIRDEST!

↑ METALLIC (ALUMINUM?)

WORN WITH THESE GLASSES.

SAFETY — IKKYU SAN'S BUDDY

← SHIMURA

LADIES STRAW HAT WORN BY A GRAMPS

MOST POPULAR WITH THE GRANNIES

SEEN: 2 boy RACERS on Jet-skis, WHO CAME From SHIRAISHISHIMA.

Good Job I Chose MANABE.

JAPANESE RUBBER-BAND GUN.

STOP TO BLOCK THE RUBBER BAND

AMMO

Rubber BAND

Swivels

TRIGGER

HANDLE

VERY Easy To build: No gLUE OR FILING, JUST 2 PAIRS OF CHOPSTICKS (hashi) WILL do AND PLENTY OF Rubber bands.

UNLike my SHŌGI EXPLANATION, THIS DRAWING SHOULD ALLOW some UNDERSTANDING OF the item AND enable PLAY.

500 YEARS ago, ON TANEGASHIMA iSLAND, the JAPANESE HAD A SINGLE obsession: To Find OUT HOW To make the STRANGE muskets and RIFLES of the PORTUGUESE who HAD JUST COME ASHORE.

5 CENTURIES Later, intrigued by A kid's Toy, A FRENCH TOURIST FRESHLY installed on Manabe Reverses HISTORY and obTains the PLANS for making A weapon JUST as imporTant for the development of his COUNTRY. At Least He Hopes.

STRANGELY enough, SHIMURA san is sure that James Bond is FRENCH.

I am Rather Glad I WAS Able To make one, but out of PiTY FOR the CATS HERE who are Already weakLings, I use it on Crabs, much guilTier in my eyes.

THIS Cat Really exists.

Ping!

10 MiNuTeS AFTeR I GeT THeRe, iT'S **TiMe To PuLL UP THe NeT**

(After Leaving it to soak For Two Hours.)

Putting on the Large gLoves.

ManaGes the KaNi

I don't know exactly what happens underwater, but here kani Are Captured with A small-holed, thick-mesh NeT.

What's Going oN?

Manages the Net.

This is when the gLoves' tHickness Comes in Handy.

Kani hoLD

Once the Net is Rewound, the FLoaters used to indicate initial Position Are Recovered.

POLYSTYRENE.

DOWN, YOU DiRTY beast

FigHts Like A swordfish.

And I Finally understand the sweater's usefulness. The kani must suspect something's up because it PuTs All its strength into the battle. A Real monster.

This For iNSTANCe, MUST HuRT.

CUTTeR

Flop

10 Crabs Captured iN one Net (A Good Catch ACCORDING To them)

It'S the BEGiNNiNG of the END FoR YOU GUYS!

Let ME GO, I KNOW YAKS, ME!

KATANA

Last Leg iN THe sHape of A Fin.

LEG-GRaBBiNG TANTŌ

Hi, How GoEs iT?

SO So.

SAMPLING the MERCHANDISE (BREKKIE BREAK)

To Each his Crab, and that works out well.

YUM

HE MUST EAT Crab everyday, but He still loves it.

He explains to me How To make rubber Clips.

And to think that I watched them battle valiantly less than a hour ago.

Feast made possible by the Convenient Presence of A Gas burner in the cabin.

GAS CARTRIDGE HERe.

Between the ages of 15 and 23, He worked for NTT in Osaka. He didn't like office work and so He started His kani business.

Diagram of a Crab

Under the gills, there are large chunks of meat, well hidden. They're the best, better than claw meat. It's the crab equivalent of the chicken oyster.

THE GILLS: APPetizing Because of their Pure white color, but NON EDiBLe.

LiD.

Lid REMOVED

Maybe influenced by the Circumstances, I found this KANI A Tad better than our spider Crabs.

"MiSo" (LIKE THE SOUP) Crab Head juiCE. VERY Good and A VerY STRONG Taste.

BURP

Do You Think He LIKED THE Crab?

NoT the GILLS At any RaTe...

After this Feast, the brother comes to pick me up and so I leave them. They have one more dip-wait-pull-the-net Routine before coming back to PORT around 11:30-12:00.

About 3 to 4 times Per sea TRip

A gift from Shimura
(honey candy)

small fish in an aquarium at the Gori-Gori
(next barbecue?)

A grandma trick: THE KATORISENKOU (insecticide incense) in a mini portable box.

A single coil.

ikkyu san's wife is a fan.

PATTERNS COPIED FROM A BOOK ABOUT MANABESHIMA, AVAILABLE AT THE TEMPLE.

The Japanese Go Swimming

Let's take the example of this little office lady: the bigger the swim ring, the better.

20 years from now, she will hate having the tan she has today!

And they like it. Especially with glow plastic.

Nowadays the Santora is full every weekend and sometimes even during the week. Customers are essentially families that come and dip their bottoms, sometimes more.

ANIMAL VARIATIONS

Fish-duck? Fidu?

I made the acquaintance of **IZUTANI SAN**

55 years old

Comes from <u>Sakai,</u> (an Osaka suburb)

Has a woman but is a bachelor.

Learned English when he was bellhop in a Kyoto luxury hotel. Now he manages a car park. (I didn't know you had to "manage" them.)

He's staying 5 days. It's a lot for a Japanese.

Izutani likes the sun, the warm sea and doing nothing. In other words, the sweet life. But one thing he deplores is the low swimming abilities of today's Japanese. When he was young, little Japanese learned directly in the sea, including methods such as these two endurance swims we're trying here:

The goal is to stay the longest.

Elbows out of the water.

ichi, ni, san, chi... hmmm...44...

Keep your knees together tight and keep them out of the water.

He reckons that there's not been a white shark in the Inland Sea for a long time. But you can find them on the Pacific Coast.
But Izutani is neither a fisherman nor a diver.

TENMA OYOGI
天馬 泳ぎ
God Horse
swim
Sort of Japanese Pegasus

TACHI 立ち **OYOGI** standing

86

DEAD KANABUN.

JAPANESE WALLS

Bamboo slats cut in two.

WHICH dictate the construction of most of the island's houses.

Japanese "Adobe" DIRT + STRAW

Coating, PLASTER

PILLAR

Sometimes the surface is of burnt wood.

RAMII KAMIKIRI

TODAY, A FIRST:
HIDEKI, the policeman, in UNIFORM!

EH EH.

WELL, it's only because he's going to OKAYAMA for some TRAINING.

POO

CAT PRINTS IN THE CONCRETE.

MAMIKO

THERE you go, these
are the umibotaru.
iT's impossible
To give a faithful
impression in drawings
or in photos.
You could just believe they're blue
glow-in-the-dark grains of salt.

Except it's NOT saLt. It's Alive. As a Matter of Fact, it Moves.

Thanks to aN expLaNaTory poster (Like A 5th-Grade science Report) that the Japanese are so taken with as sooN as there's something To expLain, i was abLe to soRT of uNderstand what it was aLL abouT.

GoT this fRoM THE SaNToRa.

MAGNiFiED HuNdReds oF TiMES.

APPAReNtLy, this is A "CRab-PLaNkToN" that you FiNd mostLy (buT Not oNLy) iN the INLaNd Sea and which is phosphoREsceNt, EspeciaLLy wheN it's stREssed ouT.

HoW To CaTch UMiBoTARu:

THE SEA — "HoTARU" → FiRefLY.

A JaR and its Lid.

INside you puT the LuRe. The best is FiSh Guts oR octopus Heads.

You then poke LittLe HoLes in the Lid and you thRead Twine in one of them.

You CLose up the whoLe thiNg. TheRe, the tRaP is Ready.

Now you dip the jaR. You Have To do this oN A summer Night.

You Rig the APPaRatus and you wait an HouR. (Let's Take the oPPoRTuNity To go Eat ouR FiSh.)

You CoMe back, it's hARvest tiMe AND, SuRPRise, the jaR is AlReady AGLoW.

The UMibotaRu hAve CoMe iN, but Not the Fish (Who Would hAve LiKed To.)

DAMN.

HeY, LeAVe SOME FoR US!

So, YoU CaN NoT oNLY ReST YouR GaZe oN THE UMiBoTaRu buT ALSo YouR FINGER. INdeed, tHeY ReaCT ESPECiALLY WHeN THeY ARE STiMuLaTed (oR RatHER SQuiSHed). THeY THeN ooZe OuT A GLoWiNG BLuE LiQuiD WiTH WhiCH YoU CaN do LoTS OF tHiNGS:

HAND PRINT

DRAW

WRITE

まなべ

BuT YoU CaN ALSo WaTCH THEM WiTHOuT CaTcHiNG THEM, if YoU PaY ATTeNTioN. EaCH diffuSE LiGHT MEANS UMiBoTaRu aRE beiNG ATTaCKed bY FiSH.

Today, SHiMuRa SaN bRouGht
Me A booK about ARt HistoRY aND
oNly SHoweD Me ReNoiR's PaiNtiNgs.

FELLOW TRAVELER →

BOAT SANPO

OR VISIT TO THE VAULTS OF MANABE'S CENTRAL BANK.

HIRONOBU ASKED IF I WANTED TO GO WITH HIM ON HIS ERRANDS. THIS LET ME GO COMPLETELY AROUND THE ISLAND BY BOAT FOR THE FIRST TIME, AND MORE IMPORTANTLY, TO DISCOVER THAT UNDER MOST PONTOONS IN HONMURA AND IWATSUBO PORTS, THERE ARE BIG NETS WITH ALL THE FISH STOCKS.

MEETING WITH A FRIEND OF HIRONOBU'S. FRESHLY CAUGHT FISH (TAI) TRANSFER.

IWATSUBO

HONMURA

SANTÓM

IN OUR SHOPPING BAG: 10 TAI, 5 TAKO AND 5 HIRAME (SOLE).

SECOND CONTROLS "IN THE FRESH AIR"

FIRST CONTROLS

TAKE THE BIG ONE, THERE. IT LOOKS GOOD.

HIRONOBU HELPS HIMSELF WHEN HE WANTS AND PAYS WHEN HE WANTS.

Kso!

Hee Hee

WHERE'S SEB?

IN THIS EXAMPLE, THERE ARE ONLY TAKO. BUT EACH NET (AND SO EACH PONTOON) HAS ITS SPECIALTY.

TAI

FLAT FISH

MEBALU

Umi no Hi

Tomorrow is The Day of the Sea across the Country.

Here we will celebrate with a small sea outing, tomorrow morning for all the island's children (I am considered a child, so I will be among them). In the meantime, tonight, there are huge preparations explained and supervised by the NPO members I met on my very first evening on the island.

DIAGRAM OF THE NET USED TOMORROW.

Right. Everybody, listen to me please, thank you. The children, Umi No Sensei and myself will be on HIROSHI san's boat while the other adults will stay on the small boat behind (in case something goes wrong), driven by ABE san the carpenter. All meet here tomorrow morning at 4 am and departure at 5 am.

Has dived with Jacques Mayol and Cousteau.

I was featured in "Thalassa" in 2001.

NAMBA san

USUI san who manages almost everything

← HIROSHI san

KATAOKA san, the grade school teacher who doesn't manage much. Anyway, he's sleeping. ↓

Okamoto san translates for me in Franglais the stuff I'm not getting.

Can you ask if 5:30 or 6 might be possible instead?

Umi No Sensei → "The Sea Professor"

He's the marine world expert. His job is to dive in all the world's seas and to share his science in the country's schools.

↳ He even dove in Odaiba (Tokyo Bay), the nut! And he saw critters there, lucky guy.

He's naturally not from here, but he came with all his gear. (Aquarium microscopes ...)

* Sort of Japanese "Atlantis" between Okinawa and Taiwan.

Work-Related Tan.

Regal bearing

Yes I know Mayol. We dove together at Yonaguni,* you know the place?

Well. A bit. Is it true that there are great white sharks in the inland sea?

Ah yes, yes. Of course. I've seen a few... They eat white dolphins, actually.

Who wants Tako?

At this hour, the sea is as calm as a lake, and as pretty as a LABU-LABU.

(Actually, i wonder if HiRoSHi's thought about this. To transform his boat into a LABU-LABU spot.)

GEO-LOCA LIZATION ACCORDING TO MY CRAB-EATER's INTUITION.

In case it's not clear, i've copied the radar image, which is self-explanatory.

★ 8 05:24 ⊙ 68° 1.7/ₛ.ₜ 28.0 v. C°

3421.626N 133 33 851E   38.6N

You ok with some music?

SEA BREAM RADIO

ENGINE PARTS?

You get in from underneath.

TELEPHONE   BATTERY?

HiRoSHi's secret garden. His boat cabin.

CASTING THE NETS

THE BOAT is STILL MOVING.

-WAITING-

SMOKE break.

The BOAT STILL MOVES SLOWLY, THEN COMES TO A STOP.

Gas at Half ←DOES NOT MOVE

HIROSHI SETS UP ROLLING PINS to guide the NETS' ROPES.

To Avoid this.

KNOTS, A FISHERMAN'S NIGHTMARE

REWINDING

The boat HARDLY moves.

WHEN THE BIG CHAINS FINALLY COME OUT OF THE WATER, HE CATCHES A ROPE THAT WAS ATTACHED TO THEM.

Net in the "UP" Direction

SPEED?

Comes UP SLOWLY

WITH THE PINS, EVERYTHING GOES FINE.

AND TAKES OFF THE SORT OF HUGE BAMBOO ROD THAT KEPT THE NET OPEN.

GAS OFF

HE TIES THE NET to A ROPE that's SUSPENDED To the MASTS AND LINKED to the "BOBBIN".

A GOOD PART OF THE NET IS ALREADY OUT

THE ROPE SQUEAKS

Net stopped

HE TIES THE ROPE FIRMLY to HOLD it.

AND RESTARTS THE NET.

Net

FIRST NET.

THE NET GOES UP MECHANICALLY AND A SMALLER NET COMES UP THAT HIROSHI IMMEDIATELY OPENS.

TAKO AND SMALL FISH.

SECOND NET.

HE TAKES OFF THE PINS.

AND THIS TIME, THE BIG NET APPEARS.

PULLS UP THE NET A bit MORE.

RETIES THE ROPE

STOPS THE NET FOR GOOD.

OPENING.

HE'S HAVING A HARD TIME.

100

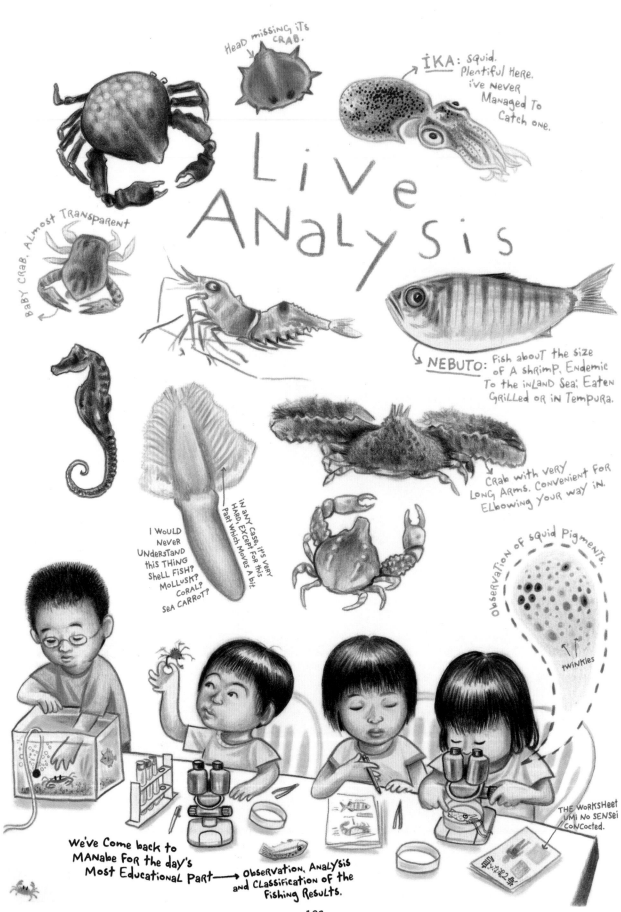

HEAD MISSING ITS CRAB.

IKA: SQUID. PLENTIFUL HERE. I'VE NEVER MANAGED TO CATCH ONE.

Live ANALysis

BABY CRAB, ALMOST TRANSPARENT

NEBUTO: FISH ABOUT THE SIZE OF A SHRIMP, ENDEMIC TO THE INLAND SEA; EATEN GRILLED OR IN TEMPURA.

IN ANY CASE, IT'S VERY HARD, EXCEPT FOR THIS PART WHICH MOVES A BIT.

I WOULD NEVER UNDERSTAND THIS THING. SHELL FISH? MOLLUSK? CORAL? SEA CARROT?

CRAB WITH VERY LONG ARMS. CONVENIENT FOR ELBOWING YOUR WAY IN.

OBSERVATION OF SQUID PIGMENTS.

TWINKLES

We've come back to MANabe for the day's most educational part → OBSERVATION, ANALYSIS AND CLASSIFICATION OF THE FISHING RESULTS.

THE WORKSHEET UMI NO SENSEI CONCOCTED.

different

HilTode

ModeLs

of sTAR FisH

BLUE'S NOT YOUR CUP OF TEA?

WE HAVE iT iN GREEN iF YOU PREFER.

UNi
(sea urchin)

STRANGE
SPECiES,
FLEXIBLE AND
LiVELY but
CAN SUDDENLY
go hard.

GoTcha!

STARFiSH WHOSE
UNDERSIDE
LOOKS LiKE
the ToP OF
that ONE.

STARFiSH
with 8 ARMS.

KANi
KAMO
(MANY
VARiATIONS)

TiNY
ANEMONES

coral

SEAWEED

HERMAN
THE
HERMiT
Crab.

Rolled out seahorse?

103

BARCODE FiSH OR SOLE FiSH (SiZE 5)

KiSU
"KISS FiSH."

"BELA" VERY
POPULAR WiTH THE
LiNE FiSHERMEN because
iT LiVES iN THE ROCKS NEAR
THE COAST.

HERMAN
THE NAKED
HERMiT CRAB.

i EAT SOME ALMOST
EVERY EVENING
AT THE SANTORA

PREPARED
LiKE THiS

VERY
difficULT to
EAT WiTH
CHOPSTiCKS.

HiRAME KAREi
SOLE   FLOUNDER
BOTH iN THE SAME FiSH:
THAT'S JAPAN FOR YOU!

104

AND DON'T TOUCH THE CUP-NOODLES, ALRIGHT?

← Toward The mini-beach SOUTH OF (HONMURA PORT.) NOT ALWAYS CLEAN.

AFTER THE THEORY COMES PRACTICE. THE CHILDREN ARE INVITED TO HUNT FOR CRITTERS in the ROCKS AS AN INTRODUCTION to diving.

I STAY IN THE COMPANY OF SOME PARENTS, HIROSHI, OKAMOTO AND Hideki, WHO discovers THE TEKO PRINCIPLe:

ON MY SNEAKER, the SMALLEST STARFISH IN the WORLD.

HEY, YOU OVER THERE. YOU ARE UNDER ARREST!

abunai?

VERY FUNNY...

COME ON, DON'T RESIST. TO THE KOBAN!

GN   GNNN

IN YOUR DREAMS!

ALRIGHT, I GOT IT. IT'S NOT FUNNY.

SPLASH

BARBECUE MAP:
(SO YOU DON'T LOSE YOUR WAY.)

SHIITAKE (MUSHROOM)

SAZAE
LARGE SHELLFISH that you MUST eat boiled instead of sashimi-style or grilled like here (Rubbery)

ALL sorts of SHRIMP (VERY salty)

KABOCHA

NASU
EGGPLANT

SORT of SLIGHTLY sweet, meaty Hotdog That kids Always Demand First.

GRILLED KISU

ONION

SHIITAKE

The good side (OR is it bad?) of the TAKO is that you Can Chew the same bit ALL Night Long. And unlike Chewing-Gum. it won't Lose its Taste.

DEMISE of the TAKO

FAMILY GEOGRAPHY

HONSHŪ

SHIRAISHI (POP. 600)

MOTHER

biG BROTHER

KITAGI (POP. 1500)

CRAZY COUSIN

ManaBe (POP. 300)

TWIN SISTER

SANAGI (POP. 300)

LITTLE SISTER

FATHER

MUJIMA (POP. 100)

SHIKOKU

IKKYU san Reads THE Newspaper.

CAT of The day:

SEEN IN A FORMER KIKU FIELD: A PHEASANT (kiji) AND ITS YOUNG.

UNDERWATER, A TAKO TRAP.

AT THE PORT, YOU FIND A LARGE NUMBER OF THESE TERRACOTTA JARS. ↓

...THAT ARE ACTUALLY TAKO TRAPS.

ON LAND, THEY'RE CAT HIDING PLACES.

WHAT'S THE VILLAGE VAGABOND'S NAME? HE WON'T TELL ME.

WHO'S THAT?

SOME SPOTS ARE SO SATURATED WITH CICADAS YOU'D THINK YOU WERE PASSING A "Miiii TREE."

AH! HIM! HE'S NOT A VAGABOND, HE'S A FISHERMAN! IT'S IWAO HANJI. BUT EVERYONE CALLS HIM ROCK.

LIKE THE STONE, NOT THE MUSIC.

mm SUITS HIM.

HYPOTHESES:

FOUND ON THE BEACH

おおつか
(有)田渕組

112

BEACH TOWEL FOR MAKI SUSHI.

まなべしま
瀬戸の香り
味付のり
走りみこし
井本水産

OBVIOUSLY A MAGNIFICENT VISUAL OF THE MANABE FESTIVAL

TODAY, I FOUND OUT ANOTHER EXPORT-RELATED ACTIVITY ON THE ISLAND:

IMOTO, THE CRAB FISHERMAN, WHO INVITED ME TO A DISMEMBERING WORKSHOP ON HIS SHIP, ALSO PRODUCES DRIED NORI (SEAWEED). IT'S VERY POPULAR IN JAPAN AND MANY REGIONS PRODUCE IT. ALONG WITH LIVE SHRIMP AND EDAMAME, THE JAPANESE HAVE MANAGED TO STAVE OFF POTATO CHIPS. GREAT HAPPY-HOUR VICTORY.

FOUND AT THE J.A. (STANDS FOR JAPAN AGRICULTURE) A HOUSE WHERE YOU CAN SELL/BUY EVERYTHING AGRICULTURE-RELATED (SEEDS, TOOLS, GOYA JAM, DRIED PLUMS AND EVEN POSTCARDS.)

HERE, IT'S EVEN BETTER WITH SHOCHO.

After having spent a few hours on the island, you understand very soon that the individual you're going to spend the most time with is him: THE FUNAMUSHI.

A funny crustacean, perfect mix of cockroach and woodlouse. Actually, i've named him the "woodroach."

Almost Human Gaze.

DOESN'T STING

They are everywhere (like crabs and mosquitoes) and they get used very quickly to the human presence (like crabs and mosquitoes).

Funamushi are our friends. We should love them too.

They love humidity but only to a point: one died in the bucket in my bathroom.

KABUTO GANI

LIST OF ITEMS THAT SHIMURA SAN HAS BROUGHT ME FROM HIS HOUSE:

- A GERMAN—JAPANESE DICTIONARY
- A ENGLISH—JAPANESE DICTIONARY
- OLD MANGA HE LOVES
- AN OLD CAMERA
- A WORLD HISTORY BOOK
- A BOOK FROM 1923
- COFFEE ICE CREAM
- A BUNCH OF TOMATOES
- MORE FISH HOOKS
- HIS BROTHER'S SKETCHBOOK
- A PAINTING OF MANABE PORT IN 1973, DONE BY HIS SECOND FAVORITE PAINTER AFTER RENOIR, KATAOKA
- A BOX OF MITSUBISHI COLORED PENCILS
- A SHEET WITH SENTENCES HE WROTE IN FRENCH (i THINK HE HAS A DICTIONARY).

LOGO ON A VAN

Found on the Ground

かぎっ
きぎっ
1つひろ…

PaLm
TRee SeeDs?

TiNy LiMEs

The SCHOOL (MIDDLE SCHOOL TO BE PRECISE) CHŪGAKKOU

ONLY building ON the island that is "Famous" (RELATIVELY speaking) because ENTIRELY made out of wood.

The ELEMENTARY SCHOOL building is that Way.

BEHIND THE BUILDING, THERE ARE SMALL GARDENS AND VEGETABLE PATCHES TENDED BY THE SCHOOL CHILDREN

ENTRANCE

AMONG MIDDLE SCHOOL STUDENTS, I ONLY KNOW:
- TAKUMI (ATSUMI NAKAMURO'S SON)
- YOSHIHIRO (HIROSHI'S SON)
- KUBOTA'S DAUGHTER
AND... WELL THAT'S IT.

SMALL TEMPLE THIS WAY.

The same way that Hideki insisted i draw his Koban, WATANABE SAN, the middle school principal, insisted from early on that i draw the school. It's the pride of the whole island (ALONG WITH THE MATSURI, the Goyas and the sea bream.)

THE ONLY ONE NOT BAREFOOT INSIDE THE SCHOOL.

ONCE DONE, I WENT INTO WATANABE'S OFFICE TO SHOW HIM THE DRAWING. AND, SURPRISE, MR. TECHNOLOGY WAS ALSO THERE. I TOOK ADVANTAGE OF THE FREE DRINKS, BUT I DIDN'T GET THE GIST OF THE CONVERSATION.

LATER, A GYM TEACHER LENT ME A BOOK ABOUT MANABESHIMA THAT WAS PUBLISHED IN THE 80s. (OR EVEN EARLIER)

doZo

FOUND ON THE GROUND.

IN THE BOOK IT'S CLEAR, AMONG OTHER THINGS, THAT ONCE ALMOST ALL THE ISLAND WAS CULTIVATED. OBVIOUS WHEN YOU ALSO LEARN THAT IN THE YEAR 45 OF THE SHŌWA ERA (1971) THERE WERE STILL 1169 INHABITANTS (734 IN HONMURA AND 435 IN IWATSUBO) AS OPPOSED TO 326 NOW. THERE ARE OF COURSE FEWER PEOPLE TO FARM THE LAND. i beT the LAST MANABESHIMA RESIDENT WiLL DIE CHOKED bY A TREE.

AVANT:

MAINTENANT:

AND THERE ARE EVEN PICTURES OF HIROSHI BEFORE HE BECAME A FISHERMAN.

↖VERY YOUNG,

AND REIZO SAN TOO!

WELL, HE HASN'T CHANGED.

LOOKING INTO THE INN.

SANAGI
KITAGI
MANABE
SHIKOKU

i LiKe tHe WateRmeLon aspect of jAPAN.

HiDEKi, the PoLiceman, gave me a LitTLE ReFLecting gizmo that you can CLip on your backPack oR CLotHes so that you don't get Run over by cars.

BuT THere ARe No CARS HERE ...

While iT was my Turn, HiRonoBu TRied to Read the LittLe PRince (Bedside Reading of Many a Japanese) in FRench.

DéSHiNé MOi OUN' MOUTON

TODAY AT THE SanTORa, EVERYBODY GOT CLiPPeD.

jAPaN's GReaT!

120

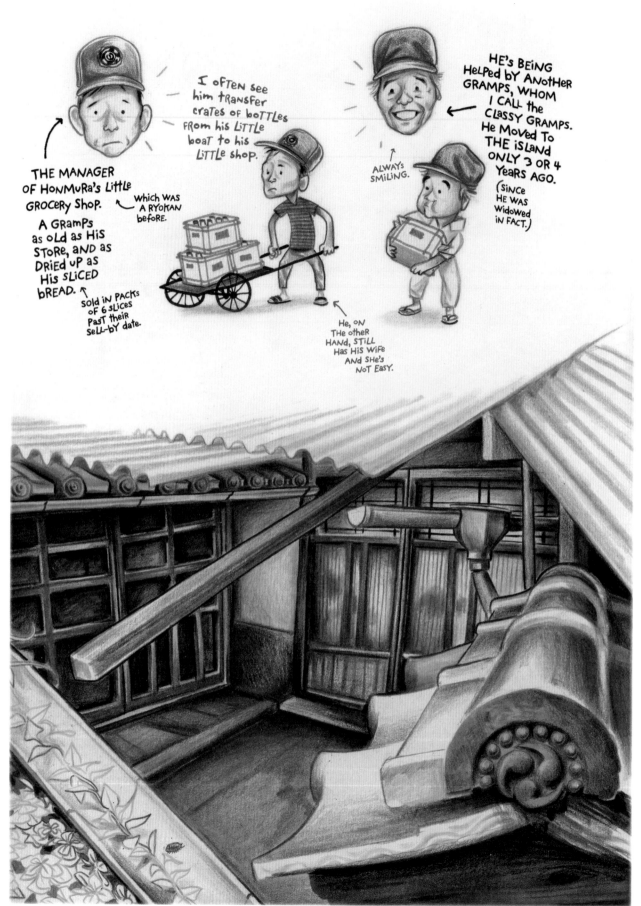

THE MANAGER OF HONMURA'S LITTLE GROCERY SHOP.

A GRAMPS as OLD as HIS STORE, AND as DRIED UP as HIS SLICED bREAD.

WHICH WAS A RYOKAN beFORE.

Sold iN PACKS of 6 sLices PasT their seLL-bY date.

I OFTEN see him tRaNSFeR cRates of boTTLes FROm his LiTTLe boaT to his LiTTLe shop.

HE's BEING HeLPed bY ANotHeR GRAMPS, WHOM I CALL the CLaSSY GRAMPS. He MoVeD To THE isLaNd ONLY 3 OR 4 YEaRs AGO.

(siNce HE WaS WidoWed iN FaCT.)

ALWAYs SMiLiNG.

He, ON THe otheR HaNd, STILL Has HiS WiFe AND SHe's NoT EaSY.

HIRONOBU'S SASHIMI

① Carefully choose the TAI according to size.

Schlack!

② Kill them with a swift blade blow behind the gills.

Repeat by the number of evening customers, at the ratio:

$\frac{1}{2}$ Tai = 1 person

Must be a crowd in tonight.

VERY VERY SHARP. ABUNAI!

③ In the kitchen, "bleed" the fish by cutting its tail with the tip of a knife.

④ Scale the fish with this efficient tool.

i end up with the chore.

SCALE FESTIVAL!

UROKOTORI

YOU'RE PUTTING EVERYTHING BACK, RIGHT?

⑤ Gut the Beast.

The Heart's still beating!

⑥ Lift the filets (so far, this is similar to normal fish preparation.)

STILL SOME SKIN, but JUST A TRACE (if I'VE done my job properly)

⑦ Dress the plate

I'M COLD.

① Bag with ice cubes.

WEDGED WITH A TOOTHPICK + PIECE OF WHITE RADISH.

③ One or more shiso leaves.

② ON the ice, shredded white radish.

⑧ Slice the filets (SWORD Master's skill.)

Press Firmly

FAILED DRAWING SINCE IN REALITY, THE HAND IS WAY CLOSER TO THE BLADE.

⑨ And dress in order to make believe that Fish naturally live in a state of SASHIMI.

LESS THAN 15 MINUTES AGO, HE WAS STILL SWIMMING WITH HIS FRIENDS.

PARSLEY

WASABI.

THERE, it's OVER!

Takes place on the Low stretch of Land between Honmura and Iwatsubo.

CHILD. Nothing to do with the dragon.

Kodomo no matsuri

The day before my departure, it's "Children's Festival." Not the official one (Kodomo No Hi) which takes place across the whole country on May 5th. No, this is one of those small, local festivals that punctuate summer and the holidays (which will soon be over).

KUBOTA daughter

HERE too TEENS DON'T WANT TO DO ORDINARY STUFF. (THEY DON'T CONSIDER THEMSELVES KODOMO) AND SO THEY WEAR A SORT OF UGLY YUKATA-PAJAMA.

Mari-juana Leaf Pattern

AND FOR AYA, Hiroshi's only daughter, it's a double party, since it's also her birthday.

4 YEARS OLD!

SUGOI!

SHE'S PALS WITH HIDEKI THE POLICEMAN'S CHILDREN.

AYA is to the Japanese Little girl what ikkyu san is to the bar owner: A perfect example.

125

THE GRANDMAS' CLUB

WELL, HE'S A GRANDPA.

HARUKI the POSTMAN AND HIS MOTHER.

HIROSH'KUN ICE IS HIS PASSION.

MINE ARE BETTER!

WATANABE SAN, RECYCLED INTO YAKISOBA PRINCIPAL.

MR. TECHNOLOGY'S Daughter

HIDEKI the POLICEMAN, HE'S THE MOST COMMITTED TO THE YAKISOBA.

(A WAY FOR HIM TO INTEGRATE?)

MORIYA ALWAYS HERE WHEN SOMETHING'S HAPPENING IN MANABE.

STARTING TO GET IN THE SWING.

やきそば
250円

PLACE YOUR BETS

Supervised by KATAOKA SAN the grade-school Teacher, A very Easy-Going Guy.

Has very dramatic Facial expressions. Fascinating To draw.

MANAMI

SHURI

SURPRISED

LAUGHING

SLEEPING

BALLOON FISHING FOR THE FUTURE TAI FISHERMEN.

Life is Good because Rinko won A Horned beetle.

SHE'S ALREADY RAISING A CICADA.

KATSuiDE
KATSuiDE
KATSuiDE
KATSuiDE
KATSuiDE
clap CLap
Kso!
KATSuiDE
KATSuiDE
KATSuiDE

MATSURI MUSIC

TANKO BUSHI
THE COAL MINE SONG.

Popular dance in Japan even where there are no mines, with a rather obvious choreography made up of bag-carrying and cart-pushing. Not very complicated but requires a minimum time of adaptation nonetheless. Sunset dance.

The grannies, a valuable asset when it comes to traditional dance.

CLap CLap ... CLap

HOTE
HOTE
×2
EACH TIME MAKING A FORWARD STEP.

MATA HOTE
×2

KATSuiDE KATSuiDE
×1 ×1
ONE MORE STEP FORWARD.

SAGATE SAGATE
×1 ×1
GOING BACKWARDS ONE STEP AT A TIME.

OSiTE OSiTE
×2
YOU PUSH AND YOU GO FORWARD.

×2
CROSS YOUR ARMS TWICE WHILE GOING BACKWARDS.

CLAP CLap ... CLap
STOP

HOW TO DANCE THE TANKO BUSHI
炭坑節

Now's **BINGO** time! This is a sport that is of particular interest to grannies.

ICHI JŪ SAN

GOJŪNI

ROKU

← THE GYM TEACHER

SANJŪHACHI

THE BOARDS ARE FREE

GUARANTEED TO WIN

NO. 180

B I N G O!

Well, I didn't win the first prize but an assortment of towels and linens (to make grannies jealous). I'd have preferred Rinko's horned beetle.

... SANJŪ ... KYŪ ... NIJŪNI

WON! Stop! The prize is mine!

Wait... Sanjūhachi that's 28, that's it. No, it's 38, but.

so that means...

MIDNIGHT Everything is packed up.

HIROSHI and MORIMOTO invite me to the "after party": a meal at the GORI-GORI.

BUT HAVEN'T WE EATEN ALREADY?!

The 2 KUBOTA sons, very proud to take charge.

They're very awkward.

The KUBOTA sons are happy to drive the van even though they're underage.

On the way back to the village, we meet SHIZUO (aka Gloomy Guy) who, while we were stuffing ourselves with YAKISOBA, spent his evening fishing and, apparently, the timing was good.

THAT WAS A REAL SMILE!

Sea Eels (ANAGO)

EVEN NEVER-ENDING Feasts come TO A CONCLUSION.
    MORIYA invited me to sLEEP AT his PARENTS' house and
since his House is ALSO ON THE WAY. KUBOTA comes ALONG.
    It's fun except tHat we're ALL more OR Less drunk and MORIYA
has trouble FINDING His own House.
            (even Though He ORGANIZES VISITS OF THE isLand FOR
                            the TOURISTS.)

AND once he's
  FOUND the way AGAIN.
MORIYA Loses his keys. IN the End. KUBOTA PUTS us up AT his.
                    AND NOT COMPLETELY satisfied
                    with their state of DRUNKENNESS.
                OUR TWO FRIENDS CONTINUE their high-FLYing
                    discussion STARTED EARLier
                    over A PLATE of shrimps.
                        Me. I've HAD it.

So FOR my
Last Night on the
isLand i couLD
Have wished for
something softer and
more COMFORTABLE, or
ELse a poeTic moment.
sLEEPing on THE SANTORA'S
PONTOON. under the
STARS and LuLLED by A
gentLe Tide.

CAT OF THE EVENING

BUT NO.
It ENDS IN
KUBOTA's kitchen with
AN AFTERTASTE OF
SHRIMP IN MY
MOLARS.

134

THe Day After

Looks Like any other day of Departure. i go back to the hotel, Gather my belongings, give Away my Fishing Rod and pet my Last Octopus.

Before Leaving, i pay one Last visit to the Person who's Followed me the most during my island stay, but who, come to think of it, Has Never invited me to His House.

SHIMURA SAN? FLO desu.

Tap Tap

To my surprise, He Asks me To come in. i'LL see only one Room in his big oLd House, but what A Room! A Real time warp. Everything seems stuck in the 60s-70s (Like His Pants.)

He didn't want me To Take Pictures and i didn't Have enough time To draw so i did it From memory NOT (difficult)

THE ONLY PAINTING, BY HIS FAVORITE PAINTER, KATAOKA (NOT the TEACHER, ANOTHER ONE.)

TV OF INDETER-MINABLE AGE, AND PERIOD TABLE

Dial Phone NOT PLUGGED IN

Cheers!
clink

SORBONNE

HIS DESK?

TATAMI OF DOUBTFUL CLEANLINESS

SAKE IN A CAN-GLASS

He offers me sake. I've Never seen Him More at Ease, SHIMURA-san.

ENTRANCE

He ALSO shows me Photos of when He was A student iN OSAKA.

NO WAY! You were A ReaL HooLigan!

HA HA! PROFESSIONAL!

135

Then it's the PROPER departure. A Few Courageous souls Come to bid me goodbye even though a storm is Coming.

Oh great, my break....

真鍋島は心のふるさと またのおこしをまってます

Reizo san (but he's here for the mail.)

MICHIRU

THE KUBOTAS

ATSUMI

She asked me to draw Postcards for the island. And I gave her the bunch of towels won the day before.

PEANUT BUTTER, BANANA & WAFFLES!

BENTO for my 3 hours on the SHINKANSEN

RINKO

Even Kingpin came all the way here. A feat, I'm very touched.

→ MANAMI

Need I say my hands are full of gifts?

136

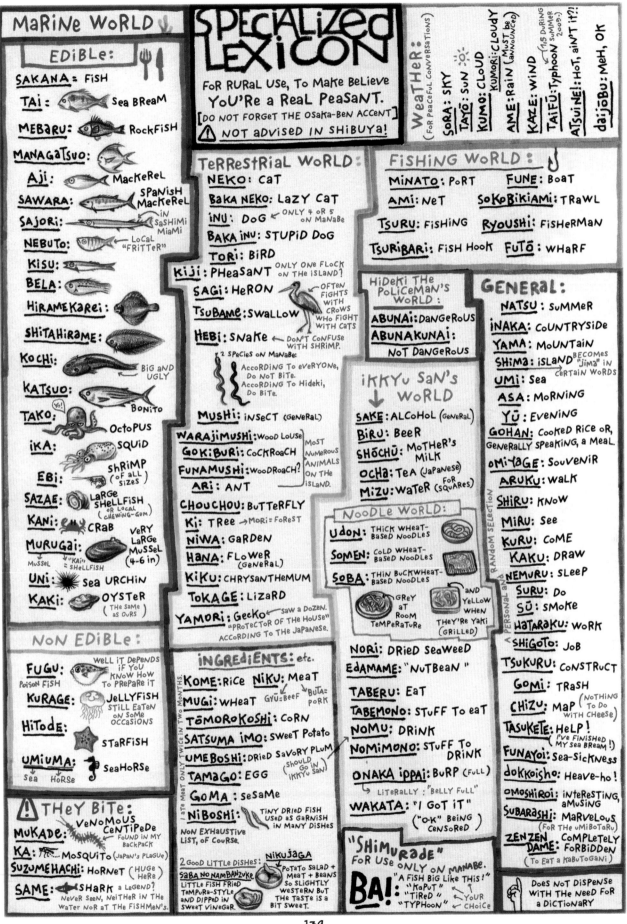

SPECIALIZED LEXICON

FOR RURAL USE, TO MAKE BELIEVE YOU'RE A REAL PEASANT.

[DO NOT FORGET THE OSAKA-BEN ACCENT]

⚠ NOT ADVISED IN SHIBUYA!

MARINE WORLD

EDIBLE:

- SAKANA = FISH
- TAI : Sea Bream
- MEBARU : RockFish
- MANAGATSUO :
- AJI : Mackerel
- SAWARA : SPANISH MACKEREL (IN SASHIMI MIAMI)
- SAJORI :
- NEBUTO : LOCAL "FRITTER"
- KISU :
- BELA :
- HIRAMEKAREI :
- SHITAHIRAME :
- KOCHI : BIG AND UGLY
- KATSUO : Bonito
- TAKO : Yo! OctoPUS
- IKA : SQUID
- EBI : SHRIMP (OF ALL SIZES)
- SAZAE : LARGE SHELLFISH (OR LOCAL CHEWING-GUM)
- KANI : CRAB
- MURUGAI : VERY LARGE MUSSEL (4-6 in) [MUSSEL "KAI" ≈ SHELLFISH]
- UNI : Sea URCHIN
- KAKI : OYSTER (THE SAME AS OURS)

NON EDIBLE:

- FUGU : POISON FISH — WELL IT DEPENDS IF YOU KNOW HOW TO PREPARE IT
- KURAGE : JELLYFISH — STILL EATEN ON SOME OCCASIONS
- HITODE : STARFISH
- UMIUMA : SEAHORSE [Sea Horse]

⚠ THEY BITE:

- MUKADE : VENOMOUS CENTIPEDE — FOUND IN MY BACKPACK
- KA : MOSQUITO (JAPAN'S PLAGUE)
- SUZUMEBACHI : HORNET (HUGE HERE)
- SAME : SHARK a LEGEND? NEVER SEEN, NEITHER IN THE WATER NOR AT THE FISHMEN'S.

TERRESTRIAL WORLD:

- NEKO : CAT
- BAKA NEKO : LAZY CAT
- INU : DOG ← ONLY 4 OR 5 ON MANABE
- BAKA INU : STUPID DOG
- TORI : BIRD
- KIJI : PHEASANT — ONLY ONE FLOCK ON THE ISLAND?
- SAGI : HERON — OFTEN FIGHTS WITH CROWS WHO FIGHT WITH CATS
- TSUBAME : SWALLOW
- HEBI : SNAKE ← DON'T CONFUSE WITH SHRIMP. 2 SPECIES ON MANABE: ACCORDING TO EVERYONE, DO NOT BITE. ACCORDING TO HIDEKI, DO BITE.
- MUSHI : INSECT (GENERAL)
- WARAJIMUSHI : WOOD LOUSE
- GOKIBURI : COCKROACH
- FUNAMUSHI : WOODROACH? — MOST NUMEROUS ANIMALS ON THE ISLAND.
- ARI : ANT
- CHOUCHOU : BUTTERFLY
- KI : TREE → MORI = FOREST
- NIWA : GARDEN
- HANA : FLOWER (GENERAL)
- KIKU : CHRYSANTHEMUM
- TOKAGE : LIZARD
- YAMORI : Gecko — saw a Dozen. "PROTECTOR OF THE HOUSE" ACCORDING TO THE JAPANESE.

INGREDIENTS: etc.

- KOME : RICE
- NIKU : MEAT [GYU = BEEF, BUTA = PORK]
- MUGI : WHEAT
- TŌMOROKOSHI : CORN
- SATSUMA IMO : SWEET POTATO
- UMEBOSHI : DRIED SAVORY PLUM (SHOULD GO IN IKKYU SAN)
- TAMAGO : EGG
- GOMA : SESAME
- NIBOSHI : TINY DRIED FISH USED AS GARNISH IN MANY DISHES

NON EXHAUSTIVE LIST, OF COURSE.

I ate meat ONLY TWICE IN TWO MONTHS.

2 GOOD LITTLE DISHES:

SABA NO NAMBANZUKE: LITTLE FISH FRIED TEMPURA-STYLE AND DIPPED IN SWEET VINEGAR.

NIKUJAGA: POTATO SALAD + MEAT + BEANS SO SLIGHTLY WESTERN BUT THE TASTE IS A BIT SWEET.

WEATHER:

(For Peaceful Conversations)

- SORA : SKY
- TAYŌ : SUN
- KUMO : CLOUD
- KUMORI : CLOUDY (MUST BE ANNOUNCED)
- AME : RAIN
- KAZE : WIND
- TAIFU : TYPHOON (7/5 DURING SUMMER 2005)
- ATSUI NE! : HOT, AIN'T IT?!
- daijōbu : MEH, OK

FISHING WORLD:

- MINATO : PORT
- AMI : NET
- TSURU : FISHING
- TSURIBARI : FISH HOOK
- FUNE : BOAT
- SOKOBIKIAMI : TRAWL
- RYOUSHI : FISHERMAN
- FUTŌ : WHARF

HIDEKI THE POLICEMAN'S WORLD:

- ABUNAI : DANGEROUS
- ABUNAKUNAI : NOT DANGEROUS

IKKYU SAN'S WORLD

- SAKE : ALCOHOL (GENERAL)
- BIRU : BEER
- SHŌCHŪ : MOTHER'S MILK
- OCHA : TEA (Japanese)
- MIZU : WATER (FOR SQUARES)

NOODLE WORLD:

- UDON : THICK WHEAT-BASED NOODLES
- SOMEN : COLD WHEAT-BASED NOODLES
- SOBA : THIN BUCKWHEAT-BASED NOODLES — GREY AT ROOM TEMPERATURE — AND YELLOW WHEN THEY'RE YAKI (GRILLED)

- NORI : DRIED SEAWEED
- EDAMAME : "NUTBEAN"
- TABERU : EAT
- TABEMONO : STUFF TO EAT
- NOMU : DRINK
- NOMIMONO : STUFF TO DRINK
- ONAKA ippai : BURP (FULL) ← LITERALLY : "BELLY FULL"
- WAKATA : "I GOT IT" ("O.K" BEING CENSORED)

GENERAL:

- NATSU : SUMMER
- INAKA : COUNTRYSIDE
- YAMA : MOUNTAIN
- SHIMA : ISLAND — BECOMES "JIMA" IN CERTAIN WORDS
- UMI : SEA
- ASA : MORNING
- YŪ : EVENING
- GOHAN : COOKED RICE OR, GENERALLY SPEAKING, A MEAL.
- OMIYAGE : SOUVENIR
- ARUKU : WALK
- SHIRU : KNOW
- MIRU : SEE
- KURU : COME
- KAKU : DRAW
- NEMURU : SLEEP
- SURU : DO
- SŪ : SMOKE
- HATARAKU : WORK
- SHIGOTO : JOB
- TSUKURU : CONSTRUCT
- GOMI : TRASH
- CHIZU : MAP (NOTHING TO DO WITH CHEESE)
- TASUKETE : HELP ! (I've FINISHED MY SEA BREAM !)
- FUNAYOI : Sea-Sickness
- dokkoisho : Heave-ho !
- OMOSHIROI : INTERESTING, AMUSING
- SUBARASHI : MARVELOUS (FOR THE UMIBOTARU)
- ZENZEN DAME : COMPLETELY FORBIDDEN (To Eat a KABUTOGANI)

A PERSONAL AND RANDOM SELECTION

"SHIMURADE" FOR USE ONLY ON MANABE.

BA! "A FISH BIG LIKE THIS!" "KAPUT" "TIRED" "TYPHOON" ← YOUR CHOICE

Does Not DISPENSE WITH THE NEED FOR a DICTIONARY

FACTS and FIGURES

AREA: 0.57 SQUARE miles
CIRCUMFERENCE: 5 miles
MAXIMUM ALTITUDE: 416 feet

MANABESHIMA
ZIP CODE 714-0037
OKAYAMA PREFECTURE KASAOKA COUNTY

G.D.P. PER INHABITANT:
60 TOMATOES, 14 MELONS, 3 CATS, 100 LBS. GOYA, 30 CABBAGES, 20 SEA BREAMS, 25 OCTOPUSES, 80 LBS. SHRIMP AND 35 SOLES.
2009 ESTIMATE

EXPORTS

FISH — SHELLFISH (SAZAE) (STILL, A BIT.)
CRABS, NORI, FLOWERS, VEGETABLES (CABBAGES, GOYA, TOMATOES and UMEBOSHI (DRIED PLUMS)) AND FRUIT
→ ESPECIALLY: FUGU TAI HIRAME (SOLE) KOCHI
OCTOPUS (WHOLE OR IN KITS)

IMPORTS
WELL, ALL the REST. (INCLUDING RICE.)

NUMBER of TEMPLES: 5
→ 2 IN IWATO
→ 1 IN HONMURA
(UNDERSTAND: PLACE of WORSHIP WHERE AT LEAST ONE PERSON CAN ENTER)

NUMBER of RESTAURANTS: 2
→ IKKYU SAN
→ RYUKA (EXPENSIVE) RESTAURANT
+ KUBOTA SAN's BENTOS
One GRANNY who hAS A TEA SHOP but oFTEN CLOSED.

NUMBER of ATMS: 7
→ 2 IN HONMURA
→ 4 IN IWATSUBO (but 2 ARE EMPTY)
→ 1 AT the SANTORA

NUMBER of VEHICLES: 10 APPROX. ← INCLUDING the MINICAR

INTERNET CONNECTIONS: 3
→ Middle School
→ The SANTORA
→ NAKAMURO FAMILY

Public RESTROOMS: 3 ← INCLUDING ONE OWNED BY IKKYU SAN.

NUMBER of dISPERSED STONE KAMI (Gods): 88

One of THE MANY ISLAND LOGOS

COLDEST MONTH: FEBRUARY, 39 F
HOTTEST MONTH: AUGUST, 86 F

DEMOGRAPHIC EVOLUTION

YEAR	HONMURA	IWATSUBO	TOTAL
1971	734	435	1169
1981	530	339	869
1989	397	274	671
1990	377	251	628
1995	334	224	558
2000	277	187	464
2005	242	148	390
2009	213	113	326

No doubt ABOUT IT, GOING DOWN

AVERAGE AGE (EVALUATED WITHOUT ANY SCIENTIFIC STUDY): 50 YEARS OLD.

BOAT SCHEDULE

KASAOKA	7:25	8:10	9:10	10:50	13:20	14:15	16:30	17:50
MANABESHIMA	8:09	9:20	9:54	11:34	14:30	14:59	17:14	19:04

POSSIBLE to CALL WATER-TAXIS (BUT VERY EXPENSIVE)

Based on A PICTURE at the SANTORA

DONE ALREADY? WELL NOW YOU CAN COUNT FUNAMUSHI!!

APPEAR IN THIS BOOK?

LITTLE GAME SO YOU CAN CARRY ON READING: HOW MANY (LIVING) CRABS

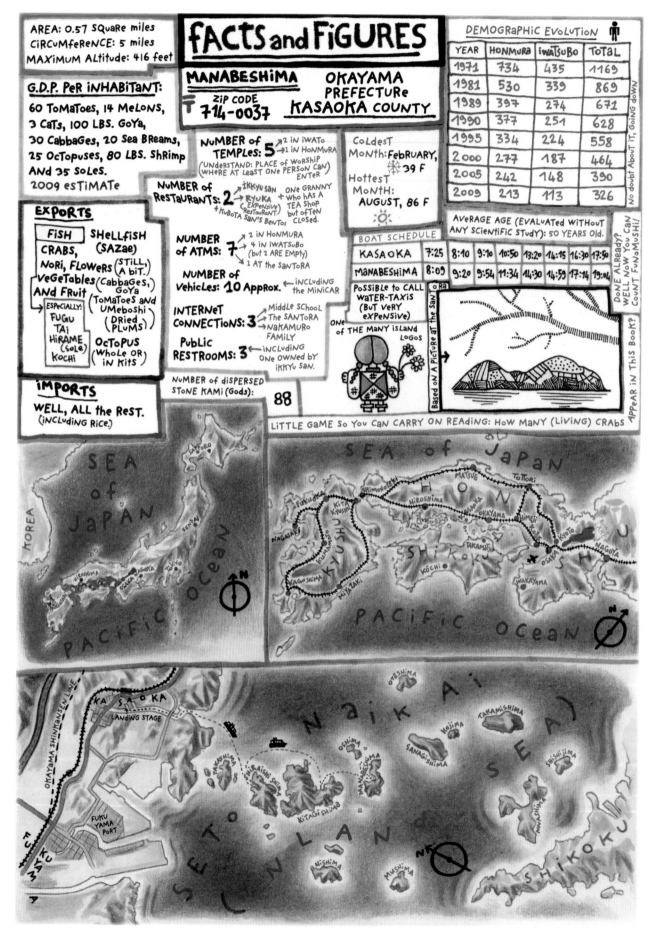

SEA of JAPAN

SEA of JAPAN

PACIFIC OCEAN

KOREA

SEDAI

HIROSHIMA OSAKA NAGOYA TOKYO

FUKUOKA KITAKYUSHU SHIMONOSEKI MATSUE TOTTORI HIROSHIMA OKAYAMA HIMEJI KYOTO NAGOYA
NAGASAKI KUMAMOTO KYUSHU TAKAMATSU SHIKOKU KOCHI WAKAYAMA OSAKA
KAGOSHIMA MIYAZAKI

PACIFIC OCEAN

OKAYAMA SHINKANSEN LINE
KASAOKA
LANDING STAGE
FUKU YAMA PORT

NAI KAI

SETO NLAND SEA

TESHIMA OSHIMA TAKAMISHIMA KOJIMA SANAGISHIMA SHISHIJIMA MANASHIMA
TAKASHIMA FUKU-AISHI SHIMA KITAGI SHIMA MANABESHIMA

NISHIMA MUSHIMA

SHIKOKU

NO FUGU WAS HURT DURING THE MAKING OF THIS BOOK.

However, the same cannot be stated about Tako, shrimp, or Umibotaru...

SOME MORE NOODLES?

HO
2009-2010